SADDLEBACK *Classics*

Hamlet

WILLIAM SHAKESPEARE

ADAPTED BY

Tom Gorman

SADDLEBACK
PUBLISHING·INC.

SADDLEBACK *Classics*

Hamlet

Julius Caesar

Macbeth

The Merchant of Venice

A Midsummer Night's Dream

Othello

Romeo and Juliet

The Tempest

Development and Production: Laurel Associates, Inc.
Cover and Interior Art: Black Eagle Productions

SADDLEBACK
PUBLISHING·INC.
Three Watson
Irvine, CA 92618-2767

Website: www.sdlback.com

ISBN 1-56254-600-7

Printed in the United States of America
08 07 06   9 8 7 6 5 4 3 2 1

CONTENTS

INTRODUCTION

About 500 years ago, Hamlet's father, the king of Denmark, was murdered by his own brother, Claudius. Then Claudius quickly married Hamlet's mother, Gertrude. As the play opens, Hamlet's father's ghost appears and tells his son who murdered him. He urges Hamlet to seek revenge. As the play unfolds, Hamlet tries to convince himself that he should murder Claudius.

This is Shakespeare's most famous play, known for the anguished character of Hamlet.

CAST OF CHARACTERS

HAMLET, PRINCE OF DENMARK Son of the dead King Hamlet, and nephew of the present King of Denmark

CLAUDIUS, PRINCE OF DENMARK Hamlet's uncle

GERTRUDE Queen of Denmark and Hamlet's mother

GHOST The ghost of Hamlet's murdered father

POLONIUS Chief adviser to Claudius

HORATIO A commoner and loyal friend of Hamlet

LAERTES Son of Polonius and the brother of Ophelia

OPHELIA Daughter of Polonius and the sister of Laertes

ROSENCRANTZ and **GUILDENSTERN** Former classmates of Hamlet

VOLTIMAND and **CORNELIUS** Danish courtiers

MARCELLUS, BERNARDO, and **FRANCISCO** Guards at the castle

REYNALDO Polonius's servant

OSRIC A Danish courtier

GRAVEDIGGERS, LORDS, ATTENDANTS, ACTORS, and **SERVANTS**

 ## ACT 1

Scene 1

*(Francisco is at his post before the castle in Elsinore. **Bernardo** enters.)*

BERNARDO: The clock has struck 12.
I'll take over the watch now, Francisco.

FRANCISCO: Thank you for relieving me.
It is bitter cold, and I am sick at heart.

BERNARDO: Has it been quiet tonight?

FRANCISCO: Not a mouse stirring.

BERNARDO: Well, good night. Tell my
Partners on watch to hurry.

FRANCISCO: I think I hear them now.

***(Horatio** and **Marcellus** enter as **Francisco** exits.)*

MARCELLUS: Hello, Bernardo!

BERNARDO: Welcome, Horatio and Marcellus.

MARCELLUS: Has it appeared again—the *thing*?

BERNARDO: I have seen nothing.

MARCELLUS: Horatio says it is only our fantasy.
He will not believe that we saw it twice!
By standing watch with us tonight, he can
See it for himself.

HORATIO: It will not appear.

BERNARDO: Sit down awhile,
And let us once again tell you about
What we have seen two nights in a row.
Last night, about this same time,
The clock was striking one—

MARCELLUS: Quiet! It's coming again!

*(The **Ghost** enters, dressed in armor.)*

BERNARDO: It looks just like the dead King!

MARCELLUS: Speak to it, Horatio!

HORATIO *(to the Ghost)*: Who are you?
Why do you wear the armor in which
Our buried King did sometimes march?
By heaven, I order you to speak!

MARCELLUS: It seems to be offended.

BERNARDO: See, it stalks away!

HORATIO: Stay! Speak! I order you, speak!

*(The **Ghost** exits.)*

MARCELLUS: It will not answer. It is gone.

BERNARDO: What do you think now, Horatio?
You tremble and look pale.
Isn't this something more than fantasy?

HORATIO: Before my God,
I would never have believed it
Unless I saw it with my own eyes.

MARCELLUS: Isn't it like the King?

HORATIO: As like as you are to yourself!
That was the very armor he had on when
He fought the ambitious King of Norway.
And he frowned just like that once,
When angry. It is strange.
I have no idea what to think.
But it seems like a bad sign.

MARCELLUS: Tell me, if you know,
Why this quiet and watchful ghost
Has come here these past nights.
And why does our country seem
To be preparing for war?

HORATIO: I'll tell what I've heard.
Our last King, whose image just appeared,
Killed King Fortinbras of Norway.
Along with his life,
Fortinbras lost all the lands
He had risked in the battle.
If Fortinbras had won, our good King
Would have had to give up his lands.
That was their agreement, so it was only fair.
Now, sir, young Fortinbras, his son,
Rash, hot, and foolish,
Has raised an army of lawless men
To recover the land lost by his father.
This must be why we are preparing for war,
And the reason we must keep watch at night.

BERNARDO: I think you must be right.

HORATIO: Quiet! Look! Here it comes again!

*(The **Ghost** enters again.)*

>Stay, illusion! If you have any use of voice,
>Speak to me. If I may help you in any way,
>Speak to me. If you know anything about
>Your country's fate, which,
>By knowing in advance, we may avoid,
>Oh, speak!

*(A rooster crows. The **Ghost** exits.)*

BERNARDO: It was about to speak,
>When the rooster crowed.

HORATIO: I have heard that spirits
>Must leave the earth during the day,
>And what we just saw proves that story!
>The sun is rising. Our watch is over.
>Let us report what we have seen tonight
>To young Hamlet. I think that
>This spirit, silent to us, will speak to him.

MARCELLUS: Let's do it. I know where he is.

*(**All** exit.)*

Scene 2

*(**King Claudius, Queen Gertrude, Prince Hamlet, Polonius, Laertes, Voltimand, Cornelius, Lords,** and **Attendants** enter a room of state in the castle at Elsinore.)*

KING: The memory of our dear brother's death
  Is still fresh. Our hearts are full of grief.
  Yet, we must think of our kingdom,
  Which needs a leader in this warlike time.
  Therefore we have taken as wife
  Our former sister-in-law.
  Now, as you know, young Fortinbras
  Thinks that we are weak. He thinks that
  Our late dear brother's death
  Has left our state in confusion and chaos.
  Thinking he has an advantage, he has been
  Pestering us to surrender those lands
  Lost by his father to our brother.
  That is the reason for this meeting.
  We have written to the King of Norway,
  The uncle of young Fortinbras.
  He is sick and bedridden. He knows little
  Of his nephew's actions. We asked him
  To order his nephew to leave us alone.
  We want you, Cornelius and Voltimand,
  To take this letter to the King of Norway.
  Now farewell—and do your duty quickly!

(King Claudius hands them a letter.)

CORNELIUS AND VOLTIMAND: Yes, my lord.

(They bow and exit.)

KING: Now, Laertes, what's the news with you?
  You mentioned a request. What is it?

LAERTES: My good lord, I ask your permission

9

To return to France. I came here willingly
To show my support for your coronation.
Now, I must confess, that duty done,
My wishes bend again toward France.

KING: Do you have your father's permission?
What does Polonius say?

POLONIUS: My lord, he has my permission.

KING: Enjoy your youth, Laertes. Time is yours,
And you may spend it as you like!
But now, my nephew Hamlet, and my son—

HAMLET *(aside)***:** I may be your nephew,
But I will never be your son!

KING: Why are you still so gloomy?

QUEEN: Good Hamlet, cast off your dark mood.
You know that all living things must die,
Passing through nature to eternity.

HAMLET: Yes, madam, I know.

KING: It is sweet of you, Hamlet,
To mourn this way for your father.
But, your father lost a father.
And that lost father also lost his.
You must mourn for a time. But to keep on
Mourning so long is stubborn and unmanly.
It shows a weak heart, an impatient mind.
It is a fault against heaven, against the dead,
And against nature. Please stop grieving.
Think of us as a father. Let all see that

You are heir to the throne, and I love you
No less than the dearest father loves his son!
Your wish to return to school in Wittenberg
Goes against our wishes. We ask you to stay
Here in the cheer and comfort of our eye,
Our chief courtier, nephew, and our son.

QUEEN: Please, Hamlet, stay here with us.

HAMLET: I shall obey you, Mother.

KING: Why, it is a loving and fair reply.
(to the Queen): Madam, come.

(All exit but Hamlet.)

HAMLET: Oh, that this too, too solid flesh
Would melt, thaw, and turn into a dew!
Or if only suicide were not a sin!
Oh, God! Oh, God!
How weary, stale, flat, and useless
The world seems! It is an unweeded garden,
Gone to seed. That it should come to this!
Not even two months dead, so fine a king!
He loved my mother so much that
He wouldn't allow the wind to blow too hard
On her face. She would hang on him
As if her appetite grew by what it fed on.
Yet, within a month—let me not think of it!
Frailty, your name is woman!
Oh, God! A beast with no power to reason
Would have mourned longer! Now,

Married to my uncle—my father's brother—
But no more like my father
Than I am like Hercules. Within a month,
Before the salt of her tears had left her eyes,
She married. Oh, most wicked speed!
This marriage can come to no good.
But break, my heart—I must hold my
    tongue!

(Horatio, Marcellus, and Bernardo enter.)

HORATIO: Hail to your lordship!

HAMLET: Hello, Horatio! What brought you
    Here from Wittenberg?

HORATIO: I came to see your father's funeral.

HAMLET: Do not mock me, fellow student.
    I think it was to see my mother's wedding.

HORATIO: Indeed, it followed soon after.

HAMLET: Thrift, Horatio! The funeral meats
    Were served cold at the marriage tables.
    I wish I had never seen that day, Horatio!
    My father!—I think I see my father.

HORATIO *(surprised)*: Where, my lord?

HAMLET: In my mind's eye, Horatio.

HORATIO: I saw him once. He was a good king.

HAMLET: He was a man, all in all.
    I shall not look upon his like again.

HORATIO: My lord, I think I saw him last night.

HAMLET: Saw who?

HORATIO: My lord . . . the king, your father.

HAMLET: My father? Let me hear!

HORATIO: Yes. Listen, I will tell you about it.
For two nights, Marcellus and Bernardo
Saw a figure like your father,
Dressed from head to toe in armor.
They told me about it in secret.
I kept watch with them the third night.
The ghostly figure came.
I *knew* your father. It looked just like him.

HAMLET: Did you speak to it?

HORATIO: I did, but it did not answer.

HAMLET: It is very strange.

HORATIO: As I live, my honored lord, it is true.
We thought it our duty to let you know of it.

HAMLET: Indeed, sirs—but it troubles me.
Are you on watch tonight?

MARCELLUS AND BERNARDO: We are, my lord.

HAMLET: He was dressed in armor, you say?

BOTH: Yes, my lord.

HAMLET: Then you did not see his face?

HORATIO: We did. He wore the visor up.

HAMLET: Was he frowning?

HORATIO: His face was more sad than angry.

HAMLET: I wish I had been there!

I will watch with you tonight.
Perhaps it will walk again. If it looks like
My noble father, I'll speak to it.
Do not tell anyone else about this.
I'll see you tonight, between 11 and 12.

ALL: Until then, farewell.

(Horatio, Marcellus, and Bernardo exit.)

HAMLET: My father's spirit—in arms! All is
   not well.
I wish night had already come! Until then,
Be still, my soul. Foul deeds will rise,
Though the earth hides them from our eyes.

(Hamlet exits.)

Scene 3

(Laertes and Ophelia enter a room in Polonius's house.)

LAERTES: My bags are on board. Farewell.
   And, sister, please write to me.

OPHELIA: Do you doubt that I would?

LAERTES: As for Hamlet, and his affections,
   Do not expect too much.
   They are like violets in the spring,
   Fast-growing and sweet, but not lasting,
   The perfume of a minute. No more.

OPHELIA: No more than that?

LAERTES: No. Perhaps he loves you now.
But be careful. Remember his position.
His will is not his own.
Unlike other people, he may not do as he
wishes.
The safety and well-being
Of this whole state depend on his choices.
Therefore, he must first consider Denmark
Before he can choose a wife.
If he says he loves you, keep all this in mind.
If you lose your heart or your honor,
You might also lose your good reputation.
Fear it, Ophelia. Fear it, my dear sister.
Be careful of the danger of desire.

OPHELIA: I shall take your words to heart.
But, my good brother, do not show me
The steep and thorny way to heaven
If you don't take your own advice.

(Polonius enters.)

POLONIUS: Still here, Laertes? Aboard! Aboard!
The wind sits in the shoulder of your sail,
And you are keeping everyone waiting.
(laying his hand on Laertes's head): There!
My blessing on you! Here is some advice.
Be friendly, but by no means vulgar.
Keep those friends you have, and
Tie them to your soul with hoops of steel.
But do not give the hand of friendship

Too easily to every new person you meet.
Give every man your ear, but few your voice.
Listen to criticism, but do not judge others.
Buy clothes as costly as you can afford—
Good quality, but not gaudy—
For a man's clothing tells a lot about him.
Neither a borrower nor a lender be,
For a loan can lose both itself and the friend,
And borrowing dulls the edge of thrift.
This above all: To your own self be true,
And it must follow, as the night the day,
You cannot then be false to any man.
Farewell. My blessings go with you!

LAERTES: I humbly take my leave, my lord.
(to Ophelia): Farewell, Ophelia. Remember
What I have said to you.

OPHELIA: It is locked in my memory,
And you yourself shall keep the key to it.

*(**Laertes** exits.)*

POLONIUS: What did he say to you, Ophelia?

OPHELIA: Something about the Lord Hamlet.

POLONIUS: I thought so.
I'm told that you and Hamlet
Have been spending much time alone lately.
If this is so, I must tell you that you do not
Understand what people might be saying.
What is between you? Tell me the truth.

OPHELIA: My lord, he has let me know
That he feels affection toward me.

POLONIUS: Affection? Ha! Are you fool enough
To believe him?

OPHELIA: He has courted me honorably
And has supported his words
With almost all the holy vows of heaven.

POLONIUS: Such vows are like traps for birds.
Do not take him seriously. From now on,
You must not be so available. In fact,
Do not spend any time alone with him.
I don't want you to even talk to him.
That's an order. Change your ways.

OPHELIA: I shall obey, my lord.

*(**Polonius** and **Ophelia** exit.)*

Scene 4

*(**Hamlet**, **Horatio**, and **Marcellus** enter an area before the castle.)*

HAMLET: The air seems to bite. It is very cold.
What is the hour?

HORATIO: I think it is almost 12.

MARCELLUS: No, it is past midnight.

HORATIO: Indeed? Then it is almost the time
That the spirit has been coming to walk.

*(The **Ghost** enters.)*

HORATIO: Look, my lord, it comes!

HAMLET: May the angels defend us!
Whether you mean us evil or good,
I will speak to you. I'll call you Hamlet,
King, Father, Royal Dane.
Oh, answer me! Tell why your holy bones
Have burst their burial clothes.
Why has your tomb opened its marble jaws
To cast you up again? What does this mean,
That you rise up to visit in full armor?
Say, why is this? What should we do?

(The Ghost motions to Hamlet.)

HORATIO: It beckons you to draw nearer.

MARCELLUS: Do not go after it!

HORATIO: No, by no means.

HAMLET: It will not speak unless I follow it.

HORATIO: Do not, my lord.

HAMLET: Why, what should I fear?
My life is not worth the price of a pin.
And for my soul, what can it do to that?
It waves me forth again. I'll follow it.

HORATIO: What if it leads you toward danger
Or into madness? Beware!

HAMLET: It waves to me still.
(to the Ghost): Go on. I'll follow you.

MARCELLUS *(holding him back)***:** You shall not go,
  my lord.

HAMLET: Hold off your hands.

HORATIO: Listen to us. You shall not go.

HAMLET: My fate cries out,
  And makes each vein in this body
  As brave as a lion.

(The Ghost beckons.)

  Let go, gentlemen.
  *(breaking free)***:** I'll make a ghost of anyone
  Who tries to stop me! I say, away!
  *(to the Ghost)***:** Go on. I'll follow you.

*(The **Ghost** and **Hamlet** exit.)*

MARCELLUS: Let us go after him.

HORATIO: What good will that do?

MARCELLUS: Something is rotten in the state of
  Denmark.

HORATIO: Heaven will take care of it!

MARCELLUS: No, let's follow him.

*(**Horatio** and **Marcellus** exit.)*

Scene 5

*(The **Ghost** and **Hamlet** enter a more remote part of
the castle.)*

HAMLET: Where will you lead me?
Speak! I'll go no further.

GHOST: Listen to me.

HAMLET: I will.

GHOST: The hour is almost come, when I must
Give myself up to the tormenting flames.

HAMLET: Alas, poor ghost!

GHOST: Do not pity me, but listen
To what I shall tell you.

HAMLET: Speak! I am bound to hear.

GHOST: And when you hear, you will be
Bound to revenge.

HAMLET: What?

GHOST: I am your father's spirit—
Doomed for a certain term to walk the night,
And for the day confined to wasting fires
Till the foul crimes done in my life
Are burned away. If I were not forbidden
To tell the secrets of my prison-house,
I could tell a tale whose lightest word
Would freeze your young blood. It would
Make your eyes pop from their sockets, and
Your hair stand up like a porcupine's quills.
But this eternal tale must not be heard
By ears of flesh and blood. Oh, listen!
If you did ever love your dear father—

HAMLET: Oh, God!

GHOST: Avenge his foul and most unnatural murder.

HAMLET: Murder!

GHOST: Murder most foul, as murder always is. But this was most foul, strange, and unnatural.

HAMLET: Tell me what happened, so that I, With wings as swift as thoughts of love, May sweep to my revenge.

GHOST: Hamlet, hear what I say. The story is being told that a serpent Stung me as I was sleeping in my orchard. All Denmark has been told this lie.

But know, noble youth,
The serpent that did sting your father's life
Now wears his crown.

HAMLET: Oh, it's just as I thought! My uncle!

GHOST: Yes, that beast.
First he won to his shameful lust
The will of my queen. Oh, Hamlet,
What a fall that was for her!
From me, whose love was sacred and true,
To that wretch who is so far below me!
But quickly: I think I smell the morning air.
I will be brief. I was sleeping in my orchard,
As was my custom in the afternoon,
When your uncle stole in upon me
And poured poison in my ear.
The poison he used was swift as quicksilver.
It coursed through my whole body
And killed me almost in an instant.
Thus, as I was sleeping, I was killed
By my own brother's hand. In one moment,
I was deprived of life, of crown, of queen.
Cut off even before I could confess my sins.
I was sent to my maker
With all my imperfections on my head.
Oh, horrible! Oh, horrible! Most horrible!
If you have any feelings in you, bear it not.
Do not let the royal bed of Denmark be
A couch for luxury and evil incest. But

Whatever you do, do not harm your mother.
Leave her to heaven and to those thorns
That lie in her heart to prick and sting her.
Farewell at once! It is almost morning.
Goodbye, goodbye! Hamlet, remember me!

*(The **Ghost** exits.)*

HAMLET: Remember you!
Yes, you poor ghost! From my memory,
I'll wipe away all foolish records,
All advice from books, all past pressures
That youth and observation put there.
Your commandment alone shall live
Within my brain, unmixed with lesser
Matter. Oh, most evil woman!
Oh, villain, villain, smiling, evil villain!
One may smile, and smile, and be a villain.
At least, I am sure, it may be so in Denmark.
So, Uncle, there you are. Now to my promise:
"Remember me." I have sworn it.

HORATIO *(from offstage)*: My lord, my lord!

MARCELLUS *(from offstage)*: Lord Hamlet!

HORATIO *(from offstage)*: Heaven help him!

*(**Horatio** and **Marcellus** enter.)*

MARCELLUS: What happened, my noble lord?

HORATIO: What news, my lord?

HAMLET: Oh, wonderful!

HORATIO: My good lord, tell us.

HAMLET: No, you will reveal it.

HORATIO: Not I, my lord, by heaven!

MARCELLUS: Nor I, my lord.

HAMLET: Then you'll keep a secret?

HORATIO AND MARCELLUS: Yes, my lord.

HAMLET: There's a villain living in Denmark.

HORATIO: We don't need a ghost, my lord,
Come from the grave to tell us this.

HAMLET: Why, you are right.
And so, let us shake hands and part.
You go about your business,
And I'll go about mine. Now, good friends,
As you are friends, scholars, and soldiers,
Grant me one poor request.

HORATIO: What is it, my lord? We will.

HAMLET: Never make known what you have
Seen tonight.

HORATIO AND MARCELLUS: We will not.

HAMLET: Swear it, upon my sword.

MARCELLUS: We have sworn, my lord, already.

HAMLET: Indeed, upon my sword, indeed.

GHOST *(from beneath the stage)***:** Swear.

HAMLET: Come on!
You hear this fellow in the cellar? Swear.

HORATIO: State the oath, my lord.

HAMLET: Never to speak of what you have seen,
Swear by my sword.

GHOST *(from beneath)*: Swear.

HAMLET: Come here, gentlemen,
And lay your hands again upon my sword.
Never to speak of what you have heard,
Swear by my sword.

GHOST *(from beneath)*: Swear.

HAMLET: Well said, old mole!
Once more, good friends.

HORATIO: Oh, this is very strange!

HAMLET: And therefore, as a stranger, welcome it.
There are more things in heaven and earth,
Horatio, than are dreamt of in your
philosophy.
But come here, as before. Swear.

GHOST *(from beneath)*: Swear.

HAMLET: Rest, rest, troubled spirit!

(Horatio and Marcellus swear.)

So, gentlemen,
With all my love I do thank you.
Let us go in together.
And, remember, not a word.
The time is out of joint. Oh, cursed spite!
That ever I was born to set it right!
Now, come, let's go together.

*(**All** exit.)*

ACT 2

Scene 1

*(**Polonius** and **Reynaldo** enter a room in Polonius's house.)*

POLONIUS: Before you visit Laertes, find out
What other people are saying about him.
You might start by saying something
Like this: "I know Laertes a little,
But not well. He seems to be very wild,
Addicted to such and such." And then you
Could name whatever vices you please, but
None so bad as to dishonor him.

REYNALDO: Such as gambling, my lord?

POLONIUS: Yes, or drinking and fighting,
The common wildness of young men.
Speak of his faults in such a way that
They may seem very minor,
The flash and outbreak of a fiery mind.
As you speak of my son's slight faults,
The person you're speaking to might say,
"I know the gentleman. I saw him yesterday,
Or the other day, or then, or then,
With such, or such. And, as you say,

There he was gambling." Listen, now,
Your bait of falsehood takes this fish of truth.
I just want to know what he's been doing.
Do you understand me?

REYNALDO: I do, my lord.

POLONIUS: Farewell now. Keep an eye on him.

(Reynaldo exits. Ophelia enters.)

POLONIUS: Ophelia! What's the matter?

OPHELIA: Oh, Father, I am so frightened!

POLONIUS: With what, in the name of God?

OPHELIA: As I was sewing in my room,
Lord Hamlet came in, his shirt unbuttoned.
He wore no hat, and his socks were dirty
And falling down to his ankles.
He had a horrible look on his face.
He seemed out of his mind.

POLONIUS: Mad for your love?

OPHELIA: My lord, I do not know.
But it seemed that way.

POLONIUS: What did he say?

OPHELIA: He held me hard by the wrist.
Then he stared directly into my face,
As if he wanted to draw it. For a long time,
He stayed like this. At last, he shook my arm,
Raised a pitiful sigh, and let me go.
Then, with his head turned over his shoulder,

He found his way out without using his eyes,
For he left my room without their help,
And, to the last, kept his eyes on me.

POLONIUS: Come with me to tell the king.
This kind of love is dangerous.
It can lead one to desperate deeds.
Have you given him any hard words lately?

OPHELIA: No, my good lord.
But, as you ordered, I've refused his letters
And have spent no time with him.

POLONIUS: That has driven him mad.
I am sorry that I misjudged him.
I thought he was toying with you and
Meant to ruin you. Maybe I am too
   jealous!
Let us see the king. We must tell him.
If this is kept secret, it could lead
To more grief than any of us need.

*(**Ophelia** and **Polonius** exit.)*

Scene 2

*(The **King**, the **Queen**, **Rosencrantz**, **Guildenstern**, and **attendants** enter a room in the castle.)*

KING: Welcome, dear Rosencrantz and
Guildenstern! We have missed you!
We asked you to come so quickly because

We need a favor from you. You have heard
Something about the changes in Hamlet.
He is different both inside and out.
The reason—other than his father's death—
I cannot imagine.
You two are close to his age and have been
Brought up with him since childhood.
I ask you both to stay here in our court
For a short time. Spend time with him.
Maybe you can find out what is wrong.
If we knew, perhaps we could help him.

QUEEN: Gentlemen, he has talked about you.
I am sure there are no two men living
That he likes any better than you.
If it will please you to spend some time here,
Your visit will be royally rewarded.

ROSENCRANTZ: No reward is necessary.

GUILDENSTERN: We are happy to help.

KING: Thank you, Rosencrantz and
Gentle Guildenstern.

QUEEN: Thank you, Guildenstern and
Gentle Rosencrantz. I beg you to visit
My too-much-changed son at once.

*(**Rosencrantz** and **Guildenstern** exit. **Polonius**
enters.)*

POLONIUS: My good lord, the ambassadors
From Norway have joyfully returned.

KING: You have always brought good news!

POLONIUS: Have I, my lord? I assure you,
Majesty, that my duty is as sacred to me
As my soul. And I think I have found
The very cause of Hamlet's madness.

KING: Oh, speak of that. I long to hear it!

POLONIUS: First, talk to the ambassadors.
My news shall be dessert to that great feast.

KING: Very well. Bring them in.

(Polonius exits.)

   (to the Queen): He tells me that he knows
Why Hamlet has been behaving so strangely.

QUEEN: I thought the reasons were clear—
His father's death and our quick marriage.

KING: Well, let us hear what Polonius says.

*(Polonius enters, with **Voltimand** and **Cornelius**.)*

Welcome, my good friends! Say, Voltimand,
What news do you have from Norway?

VOLTIMAND: The King of Norway thought
That his nephew was preparing for war
With Poland. But as he looked into it,
He found it was truly against your highness.
Then he ordered young Fortinbras to stop.
In brief, Fortinbras obeys and vows
Never to take arms against your majesty.
At this, the overjoyed King of Norway

Gave him enough money to take his soldiers
Against Poland.

(Voltimand gives the king a paper.)

The King of Norway asks your permission
For his nephew to march through your lands
On his way to Poland.

KING: When we have more time,
We'll read, answer, and think about this.
Meantime, we thank you for your efforts.
Rest now. Tonight, we'll feast together.

*(**Voltimand** and **Cornelius** exit.)*

POLONIUS: That was good news!
And now, since brevity is the soul of wit,
I will be brief: Your noble son is mad.
It is true that it is a pity,
And a pity it is that it is true.
But, to get to the point—
Let us agree that he is mad. Now we must
Find out the cause of this effect,
Or, rather, the cause of this defect.
My daughter has given me this.

(Polonius holds up a letter.)

Now, listen and think about it. *(reading)*
"To the heavenly, and my soul's idol,
The most beautified Ophelia"—
(He comments on the letter.)
That's a stupid word, a vile word.

"Beautified" is a vile word. But listen.
(reading again): "Doubt that the stars are fire.
Doubt that the sun does move.
Doubt truth to be a liar.
But never doubt that I love.
Oh, Ophelia, I am not very good at this.
But please believe that I love you best.
Oh, most best, believe it. Farewell.
I am yours forever, dear lady. Hamlet."
(He folds up the letter.)
In obedience, my daughter showed me this.

KING: But how has she received his love?

POLONIUS: Well, when I first found out about it,
I went right away and told my daughter,
"Lord Hamlet is a prince, out of your reach.
This must not be." And then I told her
That she should lock herself away from him,
Admit no messengers, receive no gifts.
She took my advice. He fell into a sadness,
Then into a fast, then into a weakness,
Then into a lightness. In this way, he fell into
The madness that all of us now mourn.

KING: Do you think this is the reason?

QUEEN: It may be. It's very likely.

POLONIUS: Have I ever been wrong before?

KING: Not that I know.
How may we test your idea?

POLONIUS: You know sometimes he walks
For hours at a time here in the lobby.

QUEEN: So he does, indeed.

POLONIUS: At such a time, I'll make sure that
My daughter is nearby.
You and I will hide behind the drapes and
Watch their meeting. If he does not love her,
And has not gone mad because of it, then
I'll quit my job and be a farmer!

KING: We will try it.

*(**Hamlet** enters, reading a book.)*

QUEEN: See how sadly he comes, reading.

POLONIUS: Go away, I beg you, both of you.
I'll speak to him presently. Please leave.

*(The **King**, the **Queen**, and **attendants** exit.)*

How are you, my good Lord Hamlet?

HAMLET: I am well, thanks to God.

POLONIUS: Do you know me, my lord?

HAMLET: Yes. You are a sly fishmonger.

POLONIUS: Not I, my lord.

HAMLET: Then I wish you were that honest.

POLONIUS: Honest, my lord?

HAMLET: Yes, sir. In this world, an honest man
Is one in ten thousand.

POLONIUS: That's very true, my lord.

HAMLET: Do you have a daughter?

POLONIUS: I have, my lord.

HAMLET: Do not let her walk in the sun.
  She could get hurt if she goes outside.

POLONIUS: What do you mean by that?
  (aside): Still talking about my daughter. Yet
  he did not know me at first. He thought
  I sold fish. He is far gone. Truly, in my
  youth, I suffered for love in much the
  same way. I'll speak to him again.
  (to Hamlet): What do you read, my lord?

HAMLET: Words, words, words.

POLONIUS: What is the matter, my lord?

HAMLET: Between who?

POLONIUS: I mean, the matter that you read.

HAMLET: Lies, sir! The writer says here that old
  men have gray beards, that their faces are
  wrinkled, and that their eyes are runny. He
  also says they lack brains and have weak
  legs. All of this, sir, I most strongly believe,
  yet I don't think it should be written down.

POLONIUS *(aside)*: Though this be madness, yet
  there is a method in it. *(to Hamlet)*: My lord,
  I must most humbly take leave of you.

HAMLET: Sir, you cannot take from me anything
  that I will more willingly give—except my
  life, except my life, except my life . . .

POLONIUS: Farewell, my lord.

(Polonius exits.)

HAMLET: These tiresome old fools!

(Rosencrantz and Guildenstern enter.)

HAMLET: Good lads, what's the news?

ROSENCRANTZ: None, my lord, but that the world's grown honest.

HAMLET: Then the end of time must be near! But your news is not true. Let me ask you a question. What have you ever done to Fortune that she sends you to prison here?

GUILDENSTERN: Prison, my lord?

HAMLET: Denmark is a prison.

ROSENCRANTZ: Then the world is one.

HAMLET: A big one, with many rooms and dungeons, Denmark being the worst.

ROSENCRANTZ: We do not think so, my lord.

HAMLET: Why, then, it is not a prison to you! For there is nothing either good or bad unless you think it so. To me, it is a prison.

ROSENCRANTZ: Then your ambition makes it one. Denmark is too narrow for your mind.

HAMLET: Oh, God, I could live in a nutshell, and count myself a king of infinite space —except that I have bad dreams.

GUILDENSTERN: Those dreams, indeed, are ambition, for ambition is merely the shadow of a dream.

HAMLET: A dream itself is but a shadow.

ROSENCRANTZ: Truly. And I believe that ambition is so light and airy that it is but a shadow's shadow.

HAMLET: Shall we go to the court? For, truly, I cannot think about this anymore.

ROSENCRANTZ and **GUILDENSTERN:** We'll wait upon you.

HAMLET: No, you won't. I will not group you with the rest of my servants. To tell the truth, I am most dreadfully waited upon. But, in the familiar way of friendship, what brings you here to Elsinore?

ROSENCRANTZ: To visit you. No other reason.

HAMLET: Thank you. But, really, dear friends, were you not sent for? Come, tell me the truth. Come, come. Speak to me!

GUILDENSTERN: What should we say, my lord?

HAMLET: Why, anything—but answer the question. You were sent for, weren't you? I know the king and queen sent for you.

ROSENCRANTZ: For what reason, my lord?

HAMLET: You tell me. In the name of our friendship, be truthful with me.

Were you sent for or not?

GUILDENSTERN: My lord, we were sent for.

HAMLET: I will tell you why, so you won't have to break your secrecy with the king and queen. I have lately—but I don't know why—lost all joy and stopped exercising. Indeed, I feel so bad that the earth seems to me a sterile place. This most excellent air—why, it seems no more to me than a foul collection of vapors. What a piece of work is man! How noble in reason! How infinite in mind! In shape and motion, how admirable! In action, how like an angel! In understanding, how like a god! The beauty of the world! The highest of animals! And yet to me, what is this piece of dust? Man does not delight me, no. Nor does woman, though by your smiling you seem to say so.

ROSENCRANTZ: I had no such thoughts.

HAMLET: Why did you laugh, then, when I said "Man does not delight me"?

ROSENCRANTZ: I was thinking, my lord, if man does not delight you, the actors who are coming will get a weak welcome.

HAMLET: Which actors are they?

ROSENCRANTZ: The ones you like so much—the tragedy-actors from the city.

HAMLET: Why are they traveling? In the city, they seemed to be doing well, in reputation and profit. Are they still as well-liked as they were when I was there?

ROSENCRANTZ: No, indeed, they are not.

HAMLET: Why? Have they grown rusty?

ROSENCRANTZ: No, they are still good. But there is a new group of child actors. They are very popular now. They are quite in fashion.

HAMLET: You say they are children? Who takes care of them? How are they fed? Will they quit acting when their voices change? Will they say later, when they grow into common actors, that their writers do them wrong?

ROSENCRANTZ: There has been much talk about it. No one knows how the argument will be resolved. Still, that is why the tragedy-actors are on the road now.

(Trumpets from offstage announce the actors.)

GUILDENSTERN: Here come the players.

HAMLET: Gentlemen, you are welcome to Elsinore. But my uncle-father and aunt-mother are deceived about me.

GUILDENSTERN: In what way, my dear lord?

HAMLET: I am but mad north-northwest. When the wind is from the south, I know a hawk from a handsaw!

(Polonius enters.)

POLONIUS: Greetings, gentlemen!

HAMLET *(aside to Rosencrantz and Guildenstern)*: That great baby you see there is not yet out of his baby clothes.

ROSENCRANTZ *(aside to Hamlet)*: Perhaps the old man is in his second childhood.

HAMLET *(aside)*: I predict that he comes to tell me of the actors. Listen.
(to Polonius): Greetings, sir.

POLONIUS: My lord, the actors are here.

HAMLET: Is that so?

POLONIUS: Upon my honor.

(Four or five actors enter.)

HAMLET: Welcome, gentlemen! Welcome, all! *(to Polonius)*: My good lord, will you see that the players have good rooms? Let them make themselves comfortable.

POLONIUS: My lord, I will. Come, sirs.

HAMLET: Follow him, friends. We'll hear a play tomorrow.

(Polonius exits, with all the actors but the first. Hamlet speaks to the remaining actor.)

HAMLET: Can you play "The Murder of Gonzago"?

FIRST ACTOR: Yes, my lord.

HAMLET: We'll have it tomorrow night. You could, if I needed it, study a speech of some 12 or 16 lines, which I'll write and add to the play, couldn't you?

FIRST ACTOR: Yes, my lord.

HAMLET: Very well. *(pointing where Polonius has exited)*: Follow that lord, and see that you do not mock him.

(First actor exits. Hamlet speaks to Rosencrantz and Guildenstern.)

I'll see you tonight. Welcome to Elsinore.

ROSENCRANTZ: Thank you, my good lord.

(Rosencrantz and Guildenstern exit.)

HAMLET: Now I am alone.
Oh, what a rogue I am! Am I a coward?
I must be, or I would have fed all the birds
With the king's body—that bloody villain!
Oh, revenge!
I, the son of a dear father murdered,
Prompted to my revenge by heaven and hell,
Must unpack my heart with words.
Well, I have heard that guilty creatures,
Sitting at a play, have been struck to the soul
By a scene reminding them of their own acts.
Sometimes they are prompted to admit

Their evil actions. I'll have these actors
Play something like my father's murder
Before my uncle. I'll observe his looks.
If he reacts, I'll know what to do.
The ghost I have seen may be the devil.
I know the devil can take a pleasing shape.
Perhaps, due to my weakness and sadness,
He is leading me down an evil path.
I want to trust the ghost—but I can't be sure
That it was my father's spirit.
I need more proof. The play's the thing
In which I'll catch the conscience of
   the king.

(Hamlet exits.)

# ACT 3

Scene 1

*(The **King**, the **Queen**, **Polonius**, **Ophelia**, **Rosencrantz**, and **Guildenstern** enter a room in the castle.)*

KING: Didn't Hamlet tell you why he has been
  Acting so strange?

ROSENCRANTZ: He says that he feels distracted,
  But he will not speak of the cause.

QUEEN: Was he interested in any pastime?

ROSENCRANTZ: Madam, it so happened that
  We passed some actors on our way here.
  We told him about this,
  And there did seem in him a kind of joy
  To hear of it. They are at the castle now,
  And I think they have already been ordered
  To play before him tonight.

POLONIUS: It is true. He asked me to invite
  Your Majesties to attend the play tonight.

KING: With all my heart, I am very happy
  To hear that he is interested in something.
  Gentlemen, tell him that we will be there.

ROSENCRANTZ: We shall, my lord.

*(**Rosencrantz** and **Guildenstern** exit.)*

KING: Sweet Gertrude, leave us, too.
  We have sent for Hamlet so that he,
  As if by accident, may meet Ophelia here.
  Her father and I—lawful spies—
  Will watch them
  Without being seen. We wish to judge,
  By the way he acts, if he is in love or not.

QUEEN: I shall obey you.
  (to Ophelia): As for you, Ophelia, I do wish
  That your beauty is the happy cause of
  Hamlet's wildness. I also hope your virtues
  Will bring him back to himself again—
  For the honor of you both.

OPHELIA: Madam, I wish the same.

*(The **Queen** exits.)*

POLONIUS: Ophelia, walk over here.
  Read from this book of prayers
  So it won't seem strange that you are alone.
  (to the King): I hear him coming!

*(The **King** and **Polonius** exit. **Hamlet** enters.)*

HAMLET: To be, or not to be—
  That is the question. Is it nobler in the mind
  To suffer the slings and arrows
  Of outrageous fortune? Or is it better
  To take arms against a sea of troubles,
  And by fighting, end them?
  To die is to sleep—no more than that.

By this sleep we say we end the heartaches
And the thousand natural shocks
That flesh must suffer. It is an end
Warmly to be wished. To die is to sleep.
To sleep . . . perhaps to dream.
Ay, there's the rub. For in the sleep of death,
What dreams may come?
These thoughts must make us pause.
Why bear the whips and scorns of time?
Why suffer the pangs of unhappy love and
The proud man's insults,
When we might end them with a dagger?
It is because we dread what might happen
After death, that undiscovered country
From which no traveler returns.
This dread puzzles the will.
It makes us prefer to bear those ills we have
Rather than fly to others we do not know.
Thus conscience makes cowards of us all.
(He sees Ophelia.) The fair Ophelia!
In your prayers, remember my sins.

OPHELIA: My lord, I have gifts of yours that
I would like to return. Please take them.

HAMLET: No, not I. I never gave you anything.

OPHELIA: You know right well you did.
And with them such sweet words that made
The things richer. Their perfume now lost,
Take them back. For, to the noble mind,

Rich gifts turn poor when givers are unkind.

HAMLET: I did love you once.

OPHELIA: You made me believe so.

HAMLET: You should not have believed me. I loved you not!

OPHELIA: Then I was truly deceived.

HAMLET: Go to a nunnery! Why should you become a mother of sinners? Why should such fellows as I be crawling between earth and heaven? We are all scoundrels, all of us. Believe none of us. Go to a nunnery! But if you do marry, I'll give you this advice: If you are as chaste as ice, as pure as snow, you will not escape slander. Be off to a nunnery!

OPHELIA: Heavenly powers, restore him!

HAMLET: Or, if you must marry, marry a fool. Wise men know well enough how wicked you might be. I say, we will have no more marriages. Those who are married already, all but one, shall live. The rest shall keep as they are. To a nunnery—go!

(Hamlet exits.)

OPHELIA: What a noble mind has lost its reason! And I, the most wretched of ladies.
I heard the sweet music of his loving words.
Now that music is out of tune and harsh.

Oh, woe is me, to have seen
What I have seen, to see what I see!

*(The **King** and **Polonius** enter.)*

KING: His thoughts are not of love!
The way he spoke—it was not like madness.
There's something in his soul that sadness
Sits on, like a hen on eggs. When they hatch,
There will be some danger. To prevent it,
I have a plan. Hamlet will go to England.
The English king owes us some money,
And Hamlet can collect it.
Perhaps the seas, and different countries,
Will bring Hamlet back to himself.
What do you think of this idea, Polonius?

POLONIUS: It should work. But I do believe
That his grief springs from neglected love.
My lord, do as you please.
But may I suggest this:
After the play, let his mother meet with him
In private. Maybe she can get him to talk.
I'll hide in the room so I can overhear them.
If she can't uncover his grief, send him
To England—or lock him up wherever
You think would be best.

KING: It shall be so: Madness in great ones
Must not go unwatched.

*(**All** exit.)*

Scene 2

*(**Hamlet** and **certain actors** enter a hall in the castle.)*

HAMLET: Say the speech as I pronounced it to you, trippingly on the tongue. If you yell it, as many of your actors do, I'd just as soon have the town-crier speak my lines. Do not saw the air too much with your hands, but use gentle motions. It is much better to act with a smoothness. Do not be too boring, either. Use your own judgment. Suit the action to the word, the word to the action. Remember that the purpose of acting is to hold the mirror up to nature. In other words, show things as they are. Now go and get ready.

*(**Actors** exit. **Horatio** enters.)*

HAMLET: Greetings, Horatio!

HORATIO: Sweet lord, I am at your service.

HAMLET: Horatio, you are as sensible a man
As I have ever known.

HORATIO: Oh, my dear lord—

HAMLET: I am not saying this to flatter you. What advantage could I hope for from you? You have no wealth but your good spirits to Feed and clothe you. Why should anyone Flatter the poor? Since I could distinguish

Among men, I chose you as a friend.
Even though you have had some bad luck,
You have never complained. You take the
Bad with the good, with equal thanks.
Blessed are those that can keep on going
No matter how fate treats them.
Give me the man who is not passion's slave,
And I will hold him in my heart—
As I do you! But enough of this.
There is a play tonight before the king.
One scene in it is very close to
What I have told you of my father's death.
When you see that act on stage,
Watch my uncle. If his hidden guilt
Does not make itself known at that point,
I'll be very surprised. I, too, will keep
My eyes on his face. After the play, we will
Compare notes about what we have seen.

HORATIO: Very well, my lord.

HAMLET: I hear them coming to the play.
I must start my mad act again.
Find yourself a place to sit.

*(Trumpets are heard offstage, announcing the king and queen. **King, Queen, Polonius, Rosencrantz, Guildenstern**, and **others** enter.)*

KING: How are you this evening, Hamlet?

HAMLET: Excellent, to be sure. Like a chameleon,
I eat the air, full of promises.

You cannot feed chickens that way.

KING: You make no sense, Hamlet.

HAMLET: Nor to me, either. Are the actors ready?

ROSENCRANTZ: Yes, my lord.

QUEEN: Come here, my dear Hamlet, sit by me.

HAMLET: No, good mother. Something more attractive pulls me.

POLONIUS *(to the king)***:** Did you hear that?

HAMLET *(to Ophelia)***:** Lady, shall I lie in your lap? *(He lies down at Ophelia's feet.)*

OPHELIA *(blushing)***:** No, my lord!

HAMLET: I mean, my head upon your lap?

OPHELIA: Well, yes, my lord. You are in a merry mood, my lord.

HAMLET: Why shouldn't I be? Look how cheerful my mother looks—and my father has been dead less than two hours.

OPHELIA: No, it's been four months, my lord.

HAMLET: So long? Oh, heavens! Dead two months, and not forgotten yet? Then there's hope that a great man's memory may outlive his life by half a year!

*(Trumpets are heard offstage. A **mime show** enters. The actor king and queen very lovingly embrace. He rests his head upon her shoulder, and she lays him*

*down on a bed of flowers. Then, seeing that he is asleep, she leaves. A short time later, in comes another man. He takes off the king's crown, kisses it, pours poison in the king's ears, and exits. The queen returns, finds the king dead, and mourns loudly. The poisoner comes in again, with three or four others, seeming to mourn with her. The dead body is carried away. The poisoner woos the queen with gifts. For a while, she seems put off and unwilling, but in the end she accepts his love. All the **actors** exit.)*

OPHELIA: What does this mean, my lord?

HAMLET: It means mischief.

*(The **announcer** enters.)*

ANNOUNCER: For us, and for our play,
We hope you like what it does say,
And now we'll start, with no delay.

OPHELIA: That was brief, my lord.

HAMLET: As brief as woman's love.

*(**Actor King** and **Actor Queen** enter.)*

ACTOR KING: It has been thirty years
Since love united us in marriage.

ACTOR QUEEN: May it be thirty more
Before our love is over!
But, woe is me, you are so sick lately.
As big as my love is, my fear is just as big.

ACTOR KING: Yes, I must leave you soon, love.

You shall live in this fair world after me.
My honored and dear wife,
I hope your next husband shall be as kind—

ACTOR QUEEN: Oh, stop talking like that!
If I take a second husband, let me be cursed!
For none wed the second
But those who killed the first.

HAMLET *(aside)*: Bitter thoughts!

ACTOR QUEEN: The only reason
For a second marriage is money, not love.
It would kill my husband a second time,
When the second husband kisses me.

ACTOR KING: I know you mean that now,
But later you might break that vow.
Nothing lasts forever, so it's not strange
That even our love might someday change.
You think you'd no second husband wed,
But that might change when the first is
    dead.

ACTOR QUEEN: Dear, I swear that this is true:
The only one I'll ever love is you.

ACTOR KING: What a deep vow!
Sweet, leave me now.
    I must sleep. *(He sleeps.)*

ACTOR QUEEN: My dear, may sleep rest you,
And may nothing come between us two.

*(**Actor Queen** exits.)*

HAMLET *(to Queen)***:** How do you like it so far?

QUEEN: The lady protests too much, I think.

HAMLET: Oh, but she'll keep her word.

KING: Have you already seen this play? Is there anything offensive in it?

HAMLET: No, no! They are just acting. The poison is not real. There's no offense in the world.

KING: What do you call the play?

HAMLET: "The Mousetrap." It's based on a murder done in Vienna. Gonzago is the duke's name. His wife is Baptista. You shall see. It's a play about evil, but what of it? Your majesty and all of us with clear consciences—it can't touch us.

(First actor enters.)

FIRST ACTOR: Evil thoughts, busy hands, strong poison, and no witnesses! It's perfect! *(He pours poison into the Actor King's ear.)*

HAMLET: He poisons him in the garden for his money. The story is written in excellent Italian. Later you shall see how the murderer gets the love of Gonzago's wife. *(The king gets up.)*

OPHELIA: The king rises.

HAMLET: Why? Did something frighten him?

QUEEN *(to King)*: What's wrong, my lord?

POLONIUS: Stop the play.

KING: Give me some light. Let's go!

ALL: Lights, lights, lights!

(All exit but Hamlet and Horatio.)

HAMLET: Horatio, did you watch him?

HORATIO: Very well, my lord.

HAMLET: During the talk about the poisoning?

HORATIO: I watched him very closely.

HAMLET: Ah, ha!

(Rosencrantz and Guildenstern enter.)

GUILDENSTERN: My lord, may I have a word?

HAMLET: Sir, you may have a whole story.

GUILDENSTERN: The king, sir. He is very upset.

HAMLET: Too much to drink, sir?

GUILDENSTERN: No, my lord. He seems quite ill.
The queen, your mother, has sent me.
She wants me to tell you that she is amazed
and astonished by your behavior.

HAMLET: Oh wonderful son, who can so astonish
a mother! Did she say anything else?

ROSENCRANTZ: She wants to speak with you in
her room before you go to bed.

HAMLET: I shall obey. Now, leave me, friends.

(Rosencrantz, Guildenstern, and Horatio exit.)

It is now the very witching time of night,
When evil comes out into the world.
Now I could drink hot blood and do
Such bitter business that the day would
Shake to look at it. Now to my mother—
Oh, heart, do not lose your nature.
Let me be cruel to her, not unnatural.
I will speak daggers to her, but use none.
After all, she is my mother. I am her son.

(Hamlet exits.)

Scene 3

(The King, Rosencrantz, and Guildenstern enter a room in the castle.)

KING: I don't like him, and I don't feel safe
Around him when he is mad. Therefore,
Prepare to go to England with him.

GUILDENSTERN: Yes, your majesty.
It is our sacred duty to keep you safe,
For so many people depend on you.

KING: Get ready for this speedy voyage.
We will put chains around this fear
Which now runs about so freely.

(Rosencrantz and Guildenstern exit. Polonius enters.)

POLONIUS: He's going to his mother's room.
Behind the drapes I'll hide and listen.
I'm sure she'll find out what's wrong.
Before you go to bed I'll call on you
And tell you what I know.

KING: Thanks, my dear sir.

(Polonius exits.)

Oh, my crime is terrible! It smells to heaven!
Like Cain in the Bible story, I have
Murdered my own brother! I cannot pray,
Though I want to so badly.
My stronger guilt defeats my strong desire.
Like a man with two things to do,
I stand here, wondering where to begin
And neglect both. This cursed hand seems
Thicker than itself with brother's blood.
Is there not rain enough in the heavens
To wash it white as snow? What prayer
Could I use? "Forgive me my foul murder"?
That cannot be, since I still have
All those things for which I did the murder:
My crown, my ambition, and my queen.
May one be pardoned and keep the goods?
In this evil world, money buys justice.
It can often buy the law, too. But it is not so
In heaven. No trickery there. What then?
What happens when one cannot repent?
Oh, wretched state! Oh, soul black as death!

Bow, stubborn knees! And, heart like steel,
Be soft as a newborn babe's skin!
All may be well.

*(The King kneels. **Hamlet** enters.)*

HAMLET *(aside)*: Now I could easily do it.
(He draws his sword.) But, no!
If I do it now, he goes to heaven.
A villain kills my father, and for that,
I, his only son, send the villain to heaven.
Oh, this would be foolish, not revenge!
He took my father by surprise,
With all his crimes on his head, lusty as May.
How his record stands, only heaven knows.
No. Up, sword, and be ready later,
When he is drunk, in his rage,
Or in the evil pleasure of his bed.
Gambling, or swearing, or doing something
That does not lead to heaven. Then get him,
So his heels may kick at heaven and his soul
May go to hell, where it belongs.

*(**Hamlet** exits. The King rises.)*

KING: My words fly up,
But my thoughts remain below.
Words without thoughts never to heaven go.

*(The **King** exits.)*

Scene 4

*(The **Queen** and **Polonius** enter her room.)*

POLONIUS: He is on his way. Now, be firm.
Tell him his pranks have been out of hand.
Say that you have spared him trouble until
now. I'll hide here silently.

HAMLET *(from offstage):* Mother, Mother!

QUEEN: Hide! I hear him coming.

*(Polonius hides behind the drapes. **Hamlet** enters.)*

HAMLET: Now, Mother, what's the matter?

QUEEN *(referring to King Claudius):* Hamlet, you
have offended your father.

HAMLET *(referring to the dead King Hamlet):*
Mother, *you* have offended my father.

QUEEN: Come, come, you answer with an idle
tongue.

HAMLET: Go, go, *you* question with a wicked
tongue!

QUEEN: Have you forgotten who I am?

HAMLET: Of course not. You are the queen,
Your husband's brother's wife, and—
I wish it were not so—you are my mother.

QUEEN: Don't speak to me like that!

HAMLET: Come, come, sit down. Do not move.

Sit here until I set up a mirror where you
May see the innermost part of yourself.

QUEEN: What will you do? Murder me?
Help, help!

POLONIUS *(from behind the drapes)***:** Help!

HAMLET *(drawing his sword)***:** What's that—a rat?
(He stabs through the drapes.)

POLONIUS: Oh, I am killed! *(Polonius dies.)*

QUEEN: Oh, my, what have you done?

HAMLET: I don't know. Is it the king?

(Hamlet draws forth Polonius.)

QUEEN: Oh, what a rash and bloody deed!

HAMLET: Almost as bad, good Mother,
As killing a king and marrying his brother.

QUEEN: Killing a king?

HAMLET: Yes, lady, that's what I said.
*(to Polonius)***:** You wretched fool, farewell!
I thought you were the king. You found out
That being too busy is dangerous.
*(to the queen)***:** Stop wringing your hands.
Sit down, and let me wring your heart.
For so I shall, unless it has become too hard.

QUEEN: What have I done, that you dare
Wag your tongue so rudely against me?

HAMLET: An act that takes the rose
From the fair forehead of an innocent love

And sets a blister there. An act that makes
Marriage vows as false as gamblers' oaths.
All of heaven is sick from thinking about it.

QUEEN: What act? What do you mean?

HAMLET: Think about your husband, so good
That he was almost like a god.
Now look at your present husband.
Do you have eyes?
You cannot call it love, for at your age,
The passion in the blood is tame.
Who would go from my father to his
    own brother?
What devil fooled you into doing it?
Oh, shame! Where is your blush?

QUEEN: Oh, Hamlet, speak no more.
  You turn my eyes into my very soul.
  There I see such black and grained spots
  That will never come clean.
  I beg you, say no more!
  These words are like daggers in my ears.
  No more, sweet Hamlet.

HAMLET: He is a murderer and a villain,
  A wretch not worth a twentieth of a tenth
  Of your former husband. A monster who
  Stole the crown and put it in his pocket!

QUEEN: No more!

HAMLET: A king of rags and patches!

*(The **Ghost** enters, visible only to Hamlet.)*

  Save me and hover over me, you angels!
  (to the Ghost): What is it, your grace?

QUEEN: Oh, no, he's mad!

HAMLET: Have you come to scold your son
  Who has not yet taken revenge? Tell me!

GHOST: Do not forget. This visit
  Is meant to push you a little.
  But, look at your mother. She suffers.
  Step between her and her fighting soul.
  Speak to her, Hamlet.

HAMLET: How is it with you, lady?

QUEEN: No, how is it with you?
  You look at nothing and speak to the air?

What are you looking at?

HAMLET: At him, at *him*! See how pale he is!

QUEEN: Dear son, nothing is there.

HAMLET: Do you see nothing there?

QUEEN: Nothing at all.

HAMLET: Did you hear nothing?

QUEEN: No, nothing but ourselves.

HAMLET: Why, look there!
See how it steals away!
My father, dressed as when he was alive.
Look—he is going out the door now!

*(The **Ghost** exits.)*

QUEEN: You are seeing things that don't exist.

HAMLET: Mother, confess your sins to heaven.
Repent what's past. Avoid what is to come.

QUEEN: Son, you have broken my heart in two.

HAMLET: Then throw away the worse part
And live more purely with the other half.
Good night. But do not go to my uncle's
bed.
Pretend to be good, even if you are not.
Stay away tonight, and that
Will make it easier tomorrow night.
The next night, it will be even easier.
(pointing to Polonius): For this, I am sorry,
But it has pleased heaven

To punish me with this, and this with me.
I will answer for the death I gave him.
So again, good night.
I must be cruel, only to be kind—
Thus bad begins, and worse remains behind.
But one more thing, good lady . . .

QUEEN: What is it?

HAMLET: I must go to England. Did you know?

QUEEN: I had forgotten. But, yes, you are right.

HAMLET: My two friends—whom I trust as I
Trust poisonous snakes—will go with me
To deliver sealed letters from the king.
So be it. It's fun to see the hangman hanged
With his own noose. I know the plan,
And they won't be able to get the best of me.
(pointing to Polonius): I'll drag the body out.
Indeed, this adviser is now so still, so grave,
Who was in life a foolish old knave.
Good night, Mother.

*(**All** exit, Hamlet dragging out Polonius.)*

ACT 4

Scene 1

*(The **King** enters a room in the castle, joining the Queen, who is groaning.)*

KING: These sighs must mean something.

QUEEN: Oh, what I have seen tonight!

KING: What, Gertrude? How is Hamlet?

QUEEN: Mad as the wind in a storm.
He heard a noise from behind the drapes,
Cried out, "A rat," and killed Polonius!

KING: Oh, heavy deed!
It would have been my fate, if I'd been there.
How will we explain this bloody deed?
The people will blame us. Where is he?

QUEEN: He has taken away the body.

KING: Oh, Gertrude, we have to find him.
We'll put him on a ship right away.
This vile deed must somehow be explained.

(Rosencrantz and **Guildenstern** enter.)*

Greetings, friends. We need some help.
In his madness, Hamlet has killed Polonius
And dragged the body away.
Go find him, and bring the body

Into the chapel. I beg you, hurry!

*(**Rosencrantz** and **Guildenstern** exit.)*

Gertrude, we'll talk to our wisest friends.
We'll let them know what has happened
And what we plan to do. Perhaps then they
Won't blame us for it. Oh, come away!
My soul is full of pain and dismay.

*(**King** and **Queen** exit.)*

Scene 2

*(**Hamlet** enters another room in the castle.)*

HAMLET: The body is safely hidden.

ROSENCRANTZ AND GUILDENSTERN *(from offstage)*:
Hamlet! Lord Hamlet!

HAMLET: Who's calling me? Here they come.

*(**Rosencrantz** and **Guildenstern** enter.)*

ROSENCRANTZ: Sir, where is the body?

HAMLET: I've mixed it with the dust.

ROSENCRANTZ: Tell us where it is, so we may
take it to the chapel.

HAMLET: Why should I be spoken to like this
by a sponge like you?

ROSENCRANTZ: You take me for a sponge?

HAMLET: Yes, one that soaks up the king's favor

and rewards. When he wants to find out
what you know, all he has to do is squeeze
you. Then, sponge, you become dry again.

ROSENCRANTZ: I do not understand you, lord.

HAMLET: I am not surprised. A good speech means
nothing to a foolish ear. Take me to the king.

(All exit.)

Scene 3

(King, with attendants, enters another room.)

KING: I have sent them to look for Hamlet
And to find the body. Hamlet is dangerous!
Yet we must not bring the law upon him.
He is loved by the people. To keep peace,
His sudden leaving must seem planned.

(Rosencrantz, Guildenstern, and Hamlet enter.)

Now, Hamlet, where's Polonius?

HAMLET: At supper.

KING: At supper! Where?

HAMLET: Not where he eats,
But where the worms are eating him.

KING: Now, now. Tell us where Polonius is.

HAMLET: In heaven. Send for him there.
If your messenger doesn't find him,
Seek him in the other place yourself.

But if you don't find him this month,
You shall smell him as you go into the lobby.

KING *(to attendants)*: Go seek him there.

HAMLET: He will stay there until you come.

*(**Attendants** exit.)*

KING: Hamlet, for your own safety, we must
Send you away with fiery quickness.
So get ready. The ship is waiting, and
The wind is high. You must go to England.

HAMLET: Good. Farewell, dear Mother.

KING: I am your loving *father*, Hamlet.

HAMLET: You are my mother.
Father and mother are man and wife.
Man and wife are one flesh.
And so, you are my mother.
Now, on to England!

*(**Hamlet** exits.)*

KING *(to Rosencrantz and Guildenstern)*: Follow him.
Make him hurry. Do not delay.
I want him out of here tonight. Away!
Everything is ready. Make haste!

*(**All** exit but the King.)*

King of England, if you value my good will,
You'll do what I ask in the letter. I want
The immediate death of Hamlet.
He rages in my blood like a sickness,

And you must cure me! Until I know it's done,
Whatever my luck, my joy will not be won.

*(**King** exits.)*

Scene 4

*(**Fortinbras** enters, leading marching forces across a plain in Denmark.)*

FORTINBRAS *(to Captain)*: Go and greet
The Danish king. Find out if he will
Still allow us to march across his land
On our way to Poland.

CAPTAIN: Yes, my lord.

*(**All** but the Captain exit. **Hamlet, Rosencrantz,** and **Guildenstern** enter.)*

HAMLET: Good sir, whose army is that?
Who commands it, and why is it here?

CAPTAIN: It is Norway's army, sir,
Commanded by Fortinbras, the nephew
Of the King of Norway. He is on his way
To fight against some part of Poland.
We go to gain a little patch of ground
That is worth very little.

HAMLET: Why, then, the Polish king
Won't even defend it.

CAPTAIN: On the contrary, sir.
The Polish army is already there.

HAMLET: What a waste! Thousands of men
Will die for no reason. I thank you, sir.

CAPTAIN: God be with you, sir.

(Captain exits.)

ROSENCRANTZ: Are you ready to go, my lord?

HAMLET: I'll be right with you. Go on ahead.

(All exit but Hamlet.)

How everything pushes me on to revenge!
What is a man, if all he does is eat and sleep?
A beast, no more. Surely he who made us
Able to think and reason
Meant for us to use that ability.
Now, perhaps I think too much.
Maybe I am one part wisdom and
Three parts coward. I do not know
Why I say "I must do this thing,"
Unless I have the cause, the will,
The strength, and the means to do it.
The examples of others urge me on.
Look at this army, led by a tender prince.
They will risk their lives for everything,
Even for an eggshell. At least Fortinbras
Acts to avenge his father. How about me,
Then, with a father killed, a mother stained?
To my shame, I see the approaching death
Of 20,000 men. They will fight for land
Not big enough for their graves.

Oh, from this time until the end,
May all my thoughts be for revenge!

*(**Hamlet** exits.)*

Scene 5

*(The **Queen** and **Horatio** enter a room.)*

QUEEN: What does Ophelia want?

HORATIO: She speaks of her father.
Her words don't make any sense.

QUEEN: Let her come in.

*(**Horatio** exits.)*

To my sick soul, everything seems
To suggest that danger is ahead.
So full of crippling fear is guilt,
It spills itself in fearing to be spilt!

*(**Horatio** enters again, with **Ophelia**.)*

OPHELIA: Where is the beautiful queen?

QUEEN: How are you, Ophelia?

OPHELIA *(singing)*: "He is dead and gone, lady,
He is dead and gone.
At his head is green grass,
At his feet, a stone."

QUEEN: But Ophelia—

*(The **King** enters.)*

OPHELIA: Listen to this: *(singing)*:
  "His shroud is white as the mountain snow.
  He lies among sweet white flowers,
  Watered by our tearful showers."

KING: How are you, pretty lady?

QUEEN: She's obsessed with her father.

OPHELIA *(singing)*: "Tomorrow is
  Saint Valentine's day
  All in the morning time,
  And I a maid at your window,
  I'll be your Valentine.
  Then up he rose, put on his clothes,
  And opened the bedroom door.
  Let in the maid, who stayed a while,
  And was a maiden nevermore.
  She said, 'Before you asked me in,
  You promised we would wed.'
  He said, 'It's true, I would have done it,
  If you'd not come to my bed.'"

KING: How long has she been this way?

OPHELIA: I hope all will be well,
  But I can't help crying.
  To think they would lay him
  In the cold, cold ground!
  My brother shall hear of it.
  And so I thank you for your good advice.
  Come, my coach! Good night, sweet ladies.
  Good night, ladies. Good night, good night!

*(**Ophelia** exits.)*

KING *(to Horatio)***:** Follow her, will you?

*(**Horatio** exits.)*

> Oh, this poison of deep grief springs
> From her father's death. Oh, Gertrude,
> When sorrows come, they do not come
> As single spies, but as armies!
> First, her father is killed.
> Next, your son is gone. The people are upset
> By talk of Polonius's death.
> They think I had something to do with it.
> Poor Ophelia! Divided from her own mind.
> Laertes has secretly come back from France.
> He has heard rumors about his father's
>   death. *(He hears a noise from offstage.)*
> What's that? Where are my guards?

*(A **gentleman** enters.)*

GENTLEMAN: Save yourself, my lord:
> Young Laertes and his rebel force
> Have swept aside your own soldiers.
> The mob calls him "Lord." They say,
> "We have chosen! Laertes shall be king!"

(Noise is heard from offstage.)

KING: The doors are broken down!

*(**Laertes** enters, followed by **some Danes**. The **gentleman** exits.)*

LAERTES: Where is the king?
  (to his followers): Guard the door.

DANES: We will, we will.

*(The **Danes** exit.)*

LAERTES *(to the king):* Oh, you vile king,
  Give me my father!

QUEEN: Calm down, good Laertes.

LAERTES: If one drop of my blood stays calm,
  It would betray my father.

KING: Why are you so angry? Tell me!

LAERTES: Where is my father?

KING: Dead.

LAERTES: I will have revenge for my father's death!

KING: Good Laertes, in getting your revenge,
  Will you kill both friend and foe?

LAERTES: None but his enemies.

KING: Do you wish to know who they are?

LAERTES: Of course.

KING: I had nothing to do with his death.
  I am in grief for it.

DANES *(from offstage):* Let her come in.

LAERTES: What noise is that?

*(**Ophelia** enters again, wearing straw and flowers on her clothing and in her hair.)*

  Ophelia! Oh, heat, dry up my brains!

May salty tears burn out my eyes!
By heaven, your madness shall be avenged!
Dear maid, kind sister, sweet Ophelia!
Oh, heavens! Can a young maid's wits
Be as mortal as an old man's life?

OPHELIA *(singing)*: "There, at his grave—
Hey non nonny, hey nonny—
Our tears we gave—"

LAERTES: If you were still sane, you could not
Speak better for revenge.

OPHELIA *(singing)*: "Will he come again?
No, no, he is dead,
Go to your death bed,
He never will come again.
His beard was as white as snow,
He is gone, he is gone,
And all we can do is moan—
God have mercy on his soul!" *(**She** exits.)*

KING: Laertes, I share your grief.
Go now and find your wisest friends.
They shall listen to both of us and judge.
If they find me guilty, then you shall have
My kingdom, my crown, my life—
And all else that I call mine. If not,
Be patient, and we shall find a way
To make up for your loss.

LAERTES: Let this be so.
The way he died, his secret burial—

No noble rites or formal ceremony—
All these things cry out for explanation.

KING: And you shall have it.
Where the guilt is, let the great axe fall.
Now, go with me.

(All exit.)

Scene 6

(Horatio enters another room with a servant.)

HORATIO: Who wants to speak with me?

SERVANT: Sailors, sir, with letters for you.

HORATIO: Let them come in.

(Servant exits. Sailors enter.)

FIRST SAILOR: Greetings, sir. This letter comes from the ambassador who was on his way to England.

HORATIO *(reading)*: "Dear Horatio,
When you have finished reading this, arrange for these fellows to see the king. They have some letters for him. Pirates boarded our ship two days after we set sail. In the battle that followed, I boarded their ship. As soon as they got clear of our ship, I alone became their prisoner. I have been treated well. They expect a favor from me in return. Let the

king have the letters I have sent. Then
come to me as fast as you would run
away from death. I have something to tell
you that will make you speechless. I do
not want to put it in writing. These good
fellows will bring you where I am.
Rosencrantz and Guildenstern are still on
their way to England. I have much to tell
you about them. Yours, Hamlet."
(to sailors): Come with me to the king.
Then you can take me to Hamlet.

*(**All** exit.)*

Scene 7

*(The **King** and **Laertes** enter another room in the castle.)*

KING: Now you know the whole story.
After Hamlet killed your father,
He tried to kill me.

LAERTES: It appears to be true. But tell me why
You did not punish him for these crimes.

KING: For two special reasons. The queen,
His mother, lives almost for his looks.
And I love her too much to let her be hurt.
Also, the common people love him.
No matter what I said about him,
They would never have believed it.
Their anger would have turned on me.

75

LAERTES *(bitterly)*: And so I have lost a noble
    father and
    My sister has been driven to madness.
    But my revenge will come!

KING: Do not lose sleep over it. Do not think
    That I am ready to forget what happened.
    You shall soon hear more.
    I loved your father, and I love myself.
    I will have my revenge for Hamlet's crimes!

*(A **messenger** enters.)*

MESSENGER: Letters, my lord, from Hamlet.
    This one is for you. This is for the queen.

KING: From Hamlet! Who brought them?

MESSENGER: Sailors, my lord.

*(**Messenger** exits.)*

KING: Laertes, you shall hear this.
    (reading): "Your majesty, I am back in your
    kingdom. Tomorrow I would like to see you
    and tell you the reasons for my sudden and
    strange return. Hamlet." What does this
    mean? Have the others come back, too?

LAERTES: Is it Hamlet's handwriting?

KING: Yes. What does it mean?

LAERTES: I have no idea, my lord.
    But let him come.
    It warms the sickness in my heart

That I shall have my revenge so soon.

KING: Will you take my advice, Laertes?

LAERTES: Yes, my lord—as long as you
Do not advise me to let Hamlet live.

KING: I have a plan for his death.
Even his mother will call it an accident.

LAERTES: My lord, I want a hand in it!

KING: I have heard that you are good at fencing.
They say you shine at the sport. In fact,
Hamlet is jealous of your reputation and
Would like nothing more than to beat you.
Now let me ask you a question.
What would you most like to do to Hamlet

To show that you are your father's son?

LAERTES: To cut his throat in the church!

KING: Revenge could take place anywhere.
But, good Laertes, here's a better plan:
Hamlet will be told that you are here.
We'll have some men praise your skill
At fencing and make bets on who would win
In a duel—you or Hamlet. He, unsuspecting,
Will not check the tips of the swords.
It would be easy for you to choose a sword
Whose tip was not covered for safety.
Then, in one practice pass,
You can settle with him for your father.

LAERTES: I will do it!
And to make sure, I'll put some poison
On the tip of my sword. I have it already.
It is so strong that there is no antidote.

KING: Let's think some more about this.
If our plan fails, it would make us look bad.
It would be better not to try than to fail.
That is why we should have a backup plan.
Let me see . . . Ah! I have it!
As you duel, you'll both get thirsty.
When he calls for drink, I'll have prepared
A cup for him. If he by chance escapes
The poison on your sword,
He'll get it from the cup.

*(The **Queen** enters, greatly upset.)*

QUEEN: One sorrow after another—
Your sister's drowned, Laertes.

LAERTES: Drowned! Oh, where?

QUEEN: There is a willow tree by the brook.
Its leaves reflect in the glassy stream.
While making flower chains there, she
Climbed up on an overhanging tree branch
To hang her garlands from it.
The branch broke off, and she fell into the
Weeping brook. For a while, her clothes
  spread wide
And held her up like a mermaid.
But then, heavy with water, her clothes
Pulled the poor wretch to muddy death.

LAERTES: Alas, then she is drowned?

QUEEN: Drowned, drowned . . .

LAERTES: You've had too much water,
Poor Ophelia, so I'll hold back my tears.
But I'm only human. I cannot. *(He cries.)*
When these tears are gone, that will be
The last of the woman in me. *(He exits.)*

KING: Let us follow him, Gertrude.
It took all I had to calm his rage!
This sad news is sure to revive it.
Therefore, let us follow him.

*(The **King** and **Queen** exit.)*

ACT 5

Scene 1

*(A **gravedigger** and his **helper** enter a churchyard.)*

GRAVEDIGGER: Is she to have a Christian burial
Even though she was a suicide?

HELPER: That's what I heard.

GRAVEDIGGER: How can that be?
Did she drown herself in self-defense?

HELPER: The coroner said it wasn't suicide.
Maybe she's getting the benefit of the doubt
Because she was a gentlewoman.

GRAVEDIGGER: Who knows? And who cares?
All I want is a drink. Why don't you go
And get us something at the tavern?

*(**Helper** exits. **Hamlet** and **Horatio** enter, and stand at a distance. They watch as the gravedigger digs and sings.)*

HAMLET: Has he no feeling for his work?
How can he sing while he digs a grave?

HORATIO: He is so used to digging graves
That he doesn't really think about it.

HAMLET: You're probably right.
Only those who don't work very hard
Have time for dainty feelings.

GRAVEDIGGER *(singing)*: "A pickaxe
And a spade, a spade,
Dig a deep pit for the latest guest.
Bring a burial sheet for the lovely maid
Who will soon be here for her final rest."

(He hits a skull with his shovel and throws it up to the surface.)

HAMLET: There's a skull. Could it be
The skull of a lawyer?
Where are his arguments now, his cases,
His evidence, and his tricks? Why does he let
This rude man now knock him about
With a dirty shovel? Shouldn't he accuse
The brute of assault? Hmmm. This fellow
Might have been a great buyer of land.
Is this how he ends up—
With his fine head full of fine dirt?
All his deeds and legal papers would
Just about fit in this box. Must the buyer
Himself have no more room than this?

HORATIO: Not an inch more, my lord.

HAMLET: I will speak to this fellow.
(to the gravedigger): Whose grave is this?

GRAVEDIGGER: Mine, sir.

HAMLET: What man do you dig it for?

GRAVEDIGGER: For no man, sir.

HAMLET: What woman, then?

81

GRAVEDIGGER: For no woman, either.

HAMLET: Who is to be buried in it?

GRAVEDIGGER: One who *was* a woman, sir.
But, rest her soul, she's dead.

HAMLET: How careful you are with words!
How long have you been a gravedigger?

GRAVEDIGGER: I began on the day that our
Last King Hamlet defeated old Fortinbras,
Thirty years ago. It was the very day
That young Hamlet was born—
He that has been sent to England.

HAMLET: Why was he sent to England?

GRAVEDIGGER: Why, because he is mad.
He shall recover his wits there.
Or, if he does not, it won't matter much.

HAMLET: Why?

GRAVEDIGGER: No one in England will notice.
There, all the men are as mad as he.

HAMLET: Say, how long will a man lie in the
earth before he rots?

GRAVEDIGGER: Eight or nine years. *(He picks up a
skull.)* Here's a skull now. This skull has
been in the earth for twenty-three years.

HAMLET: Whose was it?

GRAVEDIGGER: This, sir, was Yorick's skull—
the king's jester.

HAMLET: Let me see. *(He takes the skull.)*
Alas, poor Yorick! I knew him, Horatio.
He was a fellow of infinite fun.
He carried me on his back 1,000 times.
I hate to think of this!
Where are your jokes now, your tricks,
Your songs, your flashes of merriment?
Not one is left to mock your grinning?
Go to my lady's room right now.
Tell her that no matter how thick she puts
On her makeup, she will end up like this.
Make her laugh at that.
Horatio, do you think Alexander the Great
Looked like this in the earth?

HORATIO: Just the same.

HAMLET: And smelled like this? Pah!
(He throws down the skull.)

HORATIO: Just the same, my lord.

HAMLET: To what lowly uses we may return,
 Horatio! Even the noble dust of Alexander
 Might end up stopping up a knot-hole.

HORATIO: You think too much, Hamlet.

HAMLET: But just consider it for a minute:
 Alexander died, Alexander was buried,
 Alexander returned to dust. The dust is
   earth.
 From earth we get clay. That very clay
 Might someday stop a hole in a beer-barrel.
 The imperial Caesar, dead and turned to clay,
 Might stop a hole to keep the wind away.
 Oh, that he who awed the world might
 Patch a wall to keep the winter wind out!
 But, that's enough for now. Look!
 Here comes the king.

*(**Priests** enter, leading a procession. The **King**, the **Queen**, **Laertes**, and **mourners** follow. **Attendants** carry a coffin.)*

 Who could be in the coffin?
 The queen is here, but so few mourners!
 This suggests a suicide. It must have been
 Someone of high rank. Let's hide and watch.

*(**Hamlet** and **Horatio** hide.)*

LAERTES: What other ceremonies will there be?

FIRST PRIEST: We have already done all we can
For her funeral. Her death was doubtful.
She should be buried in unblessed ground,
And pebbles thrown on her.
Yet here she is allowed her virgin rites,
With flowers and prayers and funeral bells.

LAERTES *(sadly)*: Can no more be done?

FIRST PRIEST: No more may be done.
We would mock the service of the dead
To give her the same respect we show
To souls who parted in peace.

LAERTES: Lay her in the earth.
From her fair and pure flesh
May violets spring! I tell you, selfish priest,
My sister will be an angel
When you lie howling below.

HAMLET: What—it's the fair Ophelia?

QUEEN *(scattering flowers)*: Sweets to the sweet.
Farewell. I hoped that you would marry
Hamlet.
I wanted to scatter flowers on
Your bridal bed, sweet maid.
Instead, I put them on your grave.

LAERTES: Oh, may countless woes fall on
The man who caused her madness!

Don't bury her until I have held her
Once more in my arms! *(He leaps into
the grave.)*
Now pile your dust on both of us!

HAMLET *(advancing)*: Who is this
Who makes such a show of his grief?

LAERTES: Who is this who comes uninvited?

HAMLET *(leaping into the grave)*: It is I, Hamlet
the Dane.

LAERTES *(fighting with him)*: Her death
Was all your fault, you monster!

HAMLET: You are wrong about that.
Take your fingers from my throat!

KING *(to some attendants)*: Pull them apart!

QUEEN: Hamlet! Hamlet!

(Attendants part them. They come out of the grave.)

HAMLET: Why, I will fight him about this
Until the last moment of my life!

QUEEN: Oh, my son, about what?

HAMLET: I *loved* Ophelia! Not even 40,000
brothers, with all their love,
Could love her as much.

KING: Oh, he is mad, Laertes!

QUEEN: For the sake of God, leave him alone!

HAMLET *(to Laertes)*: Did you come to whine?
To show your love by leaping into her grave?

Be buried alive with her, and so will I.
If you're going to rant and rave,
I'll rant as well as you!

QUEEN: This is madness.

HAMLET: Laertes, why do you accuse me?
I have always loved you like a brother.
But it doesn't matter.
You may do what you may.
The cat will mew, the dog will have his day.

(Hamlet exits.)

KING: Good Horatio, look after him.

(Horatio exits.)

(to Laertes): Be patient. Think about our talk
last night.
You'll soon have another chance to fight.

(All exit.)

Scene 2

(Hamlet and Horatio enter a hall in the castle.)

HAMLET: In my letter, I mentioned that I
Wanted to tell you some things in person.
We were on our way to England—
Rosencrantz, Guildenstern, and I.
In my heart there was a kind of fighting
That kept me awake. On an impulse—

And praise be to heaven for such
   impulses—
I got up from my bunk and left my cabin.
I wrapped my sailor's coat around me
And groped around in the dark to find them.
I finally found them asleep, and I stole
Their packet of letters. I went back
To my own room again, my fears forgetting
My manners. I opened their letters.
There I found—oh, royal treachery!—
A message from our king
To the King of England. It said that,
Upon opening the letter, without even
Taking time to sharpen the axe, the king
Was to have my head cut off!

HORATIO *(shocked)*: Is it possible?

HAMLET: Here's the letter—read it yourself.
   But do you want to know what I did next?

HORATIO: I beg you.

HAMLET: I sat down and wrote a new letter.
   In it, I mentioned how the King of England
   And the King of Denmark have always been
   Good friends. In the name of the friendship,
   I said that, without stopping to debate,
   He should put the bearers of the letter
   To sudden death. They were not to be given
   Any time to say their prayers.
   Naturally, I signed it with the name of my

Mother's husband. I had my father's
Official sealing ring in my bag.
It matches the present king's seal.
I folded the letter like the other.
I sealed it with wax and placed it safely
Back where I had found the first one.
Rosencrantz and Guildenstern never
Knew about the change. Now, the next day
Was our sea-fight, when the pirates attacked.
What happened after that, you already know.

HORATIO: So Guildenstern and Rosencrantz
Went to their deaths?

HAMLET: Why, man, they loved their work!
They are not on my conscience.
Their defeat was their own fault.
When lesser men come between the swords
Of the mighty, they take their own risks.

HORATIO: What kind of a king do we have?

HAMLET: He killed my father,
Disgraced my mother, and
Stood between me and the crown.
Then he tried to have me killed!
Wouldn't it be perfect if I could put an end
To him with my own hands?

HORATIO: He will soon learn what happened
When the King of England got your letter.

HAMLET: Yes, but meanwhile, the time is mine.

89

It doesn't take long to end a man's life.
But I am very sorry, good Horatio,
That I lost control of myself with Laertes.
I'll try to make it up to him. But, still,
His grief made mine even greater.

HORATIO: Quiet! Someone's coming.

(Osric enters.)

OSRIC: My lord, welcome back to Denmark.

HAMLET: I humbly thank you, sir.

OSRIC: Sir, his majesty asked me to tell you
That he has placed a large bet on your skill.
As you may already know, Laertes
Is a highly skilled swordsman.
It is said that no one is better than he.
The king, sir, has bet six fine horses
That you can beat Laertes in a duel.
The exact bet is this: In 12 passes,
Laertes shall not hit you more than 3 times.
Laertes, on the other hand, has said that
He will hit you 9 times out of 12.
The bet could be settled immediately
If your lordship would accept the challenge.

HAMLET: I am willing. I will win for the king
If I can. If not, I will gain nothing
But my shame and the odd hits.

OSRIC: My lord, I shall deliver your message.

(Osric exits.)

HORATIO: You will lose this wager, my lord.

HAMLET: I do not think so. Since Laertes went to France, I have been practicing. I shall win with those odds. Don't think I'm not a little nervous about it. But it doesn't matter.

HORATIO *(worried)***:** If you have any bad feelings about this, I will say that you are ill.

HAMLET: Not at all. I don't pay attention to omens and bad feelings. There is a special plan in the death of a sparrow. If death comes now, it won't come later. If it is not to come later, it will come now. In any case, it will come sooner or later. Being ready for it is all that matters.

*(The **King**, the **Queen**, **Laertes**, **lords**, **Osric**, and **attendants** carrying swords enter.)*

KING: Hamlet, shake hands with Laertes.
(The king puts Laertes's hand into Hamlet's.)

HAMLET *(to Laertes)***:** Give me your pardon, sir.
I have done you wrong. You must have heard
That I am not myself lately.
Forgive me if I offended you.

LAERTES: I accept your apology.

KING: Give them the swords, young Osric.
Hamlet, you know the wager?

HAMLET: Very well, my lord.
Your grace has bet on the weaker side.

KING: I do not think so. I have seen you both.
I think you will give Laertes a good fight.

LAERTES *(seeing that he has not been given the
poisoned sword)*: This one is too heavy.
Let me see another.

HAMLET: This one is fine for me!

*(They prepare to duel. **Servants** enter with cups of wine.)*

KING: Set the cups of wine upon that table.
If Hamlet wins, I'll drink to his health!

(They begin. Hamlet scores the first point.)

KING: I'll drink to that! Your health, Hamlet.

*(He drinks some wine. Then, as trumpets play, he
secretly puts the poison into another cup of wine and
raises it, offering it to Hamlet.)*

Have a sip yourself.

HAMLET: I'll play this bout first. Set it down
for a while. *(to Laertes)*: Come on.

(They play, and Hamlet scores again.)

KING *(to the queen)*: Our son shall win.

QUEEN: But he's out of shape and short of
breath. *(to Hamlet)*: Hamlet, take my
napkin, wipe your forehead. *(picking up the
poisoned cup that the king has set aside for Hamlet)*:
I'll drink to your good luck, Hamlet.

KING: Gertrude, do not drink!

QUEEN: I shall, my lord, if you don't mind.

(She drinks and offers the cup to Hamlet.)

KING *(aside)*: The poisoned cup! It is too late.

HAMLET *(to the queen)*: Not yet, thanks. Later.

(They continue their swordplay. Fighting fiercely, Laertes wounds Hamlet with the poisoned sword. As they fight on, they drop their swords during a scuffle. Each one accidentally picks up the other's sword. Then Hamlet wounds Laertes with the poisoned sword—just as the queen falls.)

HORATIO: Both of them are bleeding!
  (to Hamlet): How are you, my lord?

OSRIC *(to Laertes)*: How are you, Laertes?

LAERTES: Why, as a bird
  Caught in my own trap, Osric.
  I am justly killed by my own treachery.

HAMLET: How is the queen?

KING: She faints from seeing you bleed.

QUEEN: No, no! The drink, the drink!
  Oh, my dear Hamlet! I am poisoned.
  (The queen dies.)

HAMLET: Oh, villainy! Stop everything!
  Let the door be locked! Find the traitor!
  (Laertes falls.)

LAERTES: The traitor is here, Hamlet.
  Hamlet, you are killed.

No medicine in the world can do you good.
In you there is not half an hour of life.
The treacherous weapon is in your hand.
The tip had no guard, and it was poisoned.
Both of us have been wounded by it.
Here I lie, never to rise again.
Your mother's poisoned.
I can say no more.
The king—the king's to blame.

HAMLET: The point is poisoned?
Then, poison, do your work!

(Hamlet stabs the king.)

OSRIC AND LORDS: Treason! Treason!

HAMLET: Here, you villain! Finish this!
Follow my mother!

(Hamlet forces the king to drink. The king dies.)

LAERTES: It is only fair. It was all his idea.
Exchange forgiveness with me, Hamlet.
I forgive you for my death and my father's.
Forgive me for yours. *(Laertes dies.)*

HAMLET: May heaven make you free of it!
I follow you. Unhappy queen, farewell!
I am dead, Horatio. You are alive.
Tell my story to those who don't know it.

HORATIO: Don't believe that I shall live.
There's still some wine left.

HAMLET: As you are a man, give me the cup.
Let it go, by heaven, I'll have it.

(Hamlet takes the cup from Horatio.)

Oh, good Horatio,
If you ever did hold me in your heart,
Stay away from happiness for a while,
And in this harsh world
Draw your breath in pain to tell my story.

(Marching and the sound of shots are heard.)

What warlike noise is that?

OSRIC: Young Fortinbras has returned in
victory from Poland. And the
ambassadors from England have also
come with news.

HAMLET: Oh, I die, Horatio!
I cannot live to hear the news from England.
But I predict that Fortinbras will be the next
King of Denmark. He has my dying vote.
Tell him— *(He cannot finish the sentence.
The rest is silence. Hamlet dies.)*

HORATIO: There ends a noble life.
Good night, sweet prince,
May flights of angels sing you to
your rest!

*(**Fortinbras, ambassadors,** and **others** enter.)*

FORTINBRAS: What is all this?

HORATIO: What would you like to see?
If it's sorrow or woe, cease your search.

FIRST AMBASSADOR: The sight is dismal.
Our news from England comes too late.
The one who gave the order cannot hear.
Rosencrantz and Guildenstern are dead.
Now where will we get our thanks?

HORATIO (pointing to the king)**:** Not from
His mouth, even if he could speak.
He never gave the order for their deaths.
I will tell you how all this happened.

FORTINBRAS: Let us hear it without delay.
I have some rights to this kingdom,
Which I shall now claim.

HORATIO: I shall also speak of that.
But for now, let us honor these dead.

FORTINBRAS: Let four captains
Carry Hamlet like a soldier. For his funeral,
Let soldiers' music and the rites of war
Speak loudly for him. Take up the bodies!
A sight like this belongs on a battlefield.
Here it seems out of place.
Go, bid the soldiers shoot.

(A salute of guns is fired. Drums beat. The bodies are
carried out. **All** exit.)